NEW EVERY DAY

30 DEVOTIONS FOR OLDER PEOPLE BY RITA MCLAUGHLAN

God's Eternal Gifts

Other *New Every Day* titles
God's Unfailing Love
God's Great Faithfulness
God's Compassionate Heart

Copyright © 2012 Rita McLaughlan
Published 2012 by CWR, Waverley Abbey House, Waverley Lane, Farnham, Surrey GU9 8EP, UK. Registered Charity No. 294387. Registered Limited Company No. 1990308.
The right of Rita McLaughlan to be identified as the author of this work has been asserted by her in accordance with the Copyright, Designs and Patents Act 1988.
All rights reserved. No part of this publication may be reproduced, stored in a retrieval system, or transmitted, in any form or by any means, electronic, mechanical, photocopying, recording or otherwise, without the prior permission in writing of CWR.
For list of National Distributors visit www.cwr.org.uk/distributors
Unless otherwise indicated, all Scripture references are from the Holy Bible: New International Version (NIV), copyright © 1973, 1978, 1984 by the International Bible Society.
Other Scripture versions used:
GNB: Good News Bible © 1996, 1971, 1976 American Bible Society
Concept development, editing, design and production by CWR
Cover image: istock/BasieB
Printed in the UK by Linney Print
ISBN: 978-1-85345-854-5

God's provision — DAY 1
God provides strength

*I*t is God who arms me with strength and makes my way perfect.

He makes my feet like the feet of a deer; he enables me to stand on the heights.

He trains my hands for battle; my arms can bend a bow of bronze.

You give me your shield of victory; you stoop down to make me great.

You broaden the path beneath me, so that my ankles do not turn over. *2 Samuel 22:33–37*

I have found this scripture a great help and comfort as I grow older! We may not have the energy that we had when we were young but God will give us the strength we need to do what He wants us to do, whatever our age.

If we feel weak and wobbly we can ask Him for stability. If daily tasks seem hard we can trust God to help us. If we feel unable to cope we can ask Him to show us how. He will train us for the battle against the powers of darkness and we can proclaim His Word and stand upon His promises. God provides for His people exactly what they need at any time and in any situation. We only have to ask.

Prayer:
Mighty God, thank You for Your provision. I trust You to give me the daily strength for whatever You want me to do. Amen.

DAY 2

God provides food

The LORD said to Moses, 'I have heard the grumbling of the Israelites. Tell them, "At twilight you will eat meat, and in the morning you will be filled with bread. Then you will know that I am the LORD your God."' That evening quail came and covered the camp, and in the morning there was a layer of dew around the camp. When the dew was gone, thin flakes like frost on the ground appeared on the desert floor. When the Israelites saw it, they said to each other, 'What is it?' For they did not know what it was. Moses said to them, 'It is the bread the LORD has given you to eat.'
Exodus 16:11–15

The Israelites had escaped from Egypt by the miraculous parting of the Red Sea and, finding themselves in the Sinai desert, were now anxiously wondering where their food would come from. One would think that, having seen one amazing miracle, they would have been able to trust God for another, but instead the whole community grumbled against Moses and Aaron. God heard their grumbling. He already had a plan to provide food for the people and the following day they had both meat and bread to eat. Sometimes we, too, grumble about our situations instead of trusting God.

Prayer:
Almighty God, I know You love me and will always take care of me. Forgive me for grumbling. Amen.

DAY 3

God provides for every part of our lives

'Therefore I tell you, do not worry about your life, what you will eat or drink; or about your body, what you will wear. Is not life more important than food, and the body more important than clothes? Look at the birds of the air; they do not sow or reap or store away in barns, and yet your heavenly Father feeds them. Are you not much more valuable than they? Who of you by worrying can add a single hour to his life?'
Matthew 6:25–27

Jesus was talking to the crowds during His 'Sermon on the Mount'. He taught them many things about how to live, how to please God, how to serve Him alone. Towards the end of the sermon He told them how valuable they are in God's sight, more valuable even than the birds of the air. Our Father provides for His people, you and me, and Jesus emphasised that we should not worry but trust. Worrying does not help in any way. Trust God for your needs – all of them.

Action:
Is anything worrying you at the moment? Think about the words of this hymn:

> **What a Friend we have in Jesus,**
> **All our sins and griefs to bear!**
> **What a privilege to carry**
> **everything to God in prayer!**
> *Joseph Medlicott Scriven (1820–86)*

DAY 4

God provides finance

*A*fter Jesus and his disciples arrived in Capernaum, the collectors of the two-drachma tax came to Peter and asked, 'Doesn't your teacher pay the temple tax?'

'Yes he does,' he replied.

When Peter came into the house, Jesus was the first to speak '... so that we may not offend them, go to the lake and throw out your line. Take the first fish you catch; open its mouth and you will find a four-drachma coin. Take it and give it to them for my tax and yours.'
Matthew 17:24–25,27

A young friend of mine once struggled to find work and support her two teenage children. She was walking along a street one day, desperately praying for help from the Lord, when a ten pound note came blowing along the pavement onto her feet. She looked to see who could have dropped it but there was no one in sight. So she picked it up and thanked the Lord for His wonderful gift to her at that time. God can miraculously provide for His people in unexpected ways, like the coin found in the mouth of a fish in our reading today. We do not need to work out *how* God will provide for us – just believe that He will.

Prayer:
Dear Lord, I know You can provide for my needs in unexpected ways, so I thank You and praise You for Your miracles. Amen.

DAY 5

God provides livelihood

After [the resurrection] Jesus appeared again to his disciples, by the Sea of Tiberias. It happened this way … 'I'm going out to fish,' Simon Peter told [the other disciples], and they said, 'We'll go with you.' So they went out and got into the boat, but that night they caught nothing. Early in the morning, Jesus stood on the shore, but the disciples did not realise that it was Jesus. He called out to them, 'Friends haven't you any fish?' 'No,' they answered. He said, 'Throw your net on the right side of the boat and you will find some.' When they did, they were unable to haul the net in because of the large number of fish. *John 21:1,3–6*

After the crucifixion and resurrection of Jesus, the disciples were feeling bewildered and lost, wondering what to do next. Simon Peter impetuously decided to go back to his old trade of fishing, something he was familiar with. It seemed, though, that he had lost his skill, as after a whole night's fishing, the men had caught nothing. Sometimes, even after our best efforts, things don't work out as we expect. When we do things God's way, however, we can expect abundant blessing and provision.

Prayer:
Thank You, Lord, for the miracle of the fish. I commit my life and my work to You again and ask for Your abundant blessing over all that I am and do. Amen.

DAY 6

God provides a sacrifice

*S*ome time later God tested Abraham. He said to him, 'Abraham!' 'Here I am,' he replied. Then God said, 'Take your son, your only son, Isaac, whom you love, and go to the region of Moriah. Sacrifice him there as a burnt offering on one of the mountains I will tell you about.' ... Abraham took the wood for the burnt offering and placed it on his son Isaac, and he himself carried the fire and the knife. As the two of them went on together, Isaac spoke up and said to his father Abraham, 'Father?' 'Yes, my son?' Abraham replied.

'The fire and wood are here,' Isaac said, 'but where is the lamb for the burnt offering?' Abraham answered, 'God himself will provide the lamb for the burnt offering, my son.' *Genesis 22:1–2,6–8*

The story goes on to tell us that as Abraham lifted the knife to sacrifice his son, God stopped him. There was a ram caught in a bush close by and Abraham was able to offer the animal instead. God tested Abraham's obedience and when He saw that the grieving father was willing to obey Him and sacrifice his only son, Abraham didn't have to go through with it. What a story! When we obey God's commands He provides for us. This story is also prophetic – read the exciting sequel tomorrow!

Prayer:
Please help me, Father, to understand Your word and to obey You. Amen.

DAY 7

God provides forgiveness

The next day John saw Jesus coming towards him and said, 'Look, the Lamb of God, who takes away the sin of the world!' John 1:29

Praise be to the God and Father of our Lord Jesus Christ, who has blessed us in the heavenly realms with every spiritual blessing in Christ ... In him we have redemption through his blood, the forgiveness of sins, in accordance with the riches of God's grace that he lavished on us with all wisdom and understanding. *Ephesians 1:3,7–8*

The story we read yesterday would have been familiar to the Jews who lived in Jesus' time. They were used to the daily sacrifice of lambs in the Temple in Jerusalem as an offering to God. But John the Baptist recognised Jesus as the true Lamb of God who had come into the world to be offered once only as a sacrifice for the sin of the whole world. When Jesus died on the cross He opened the way to heaven for all who believe in Him. Through Him we have forgiveness and the right to be His children, part of His family, with a place in heaven.
   What a wonderful provision Jesus has made for us!

Prayer:
Thank You so much, Jesus, for dying for me on the cross, for taking away my sin and making it possible for me to enter heaven! Amen.

DAY 8

Jesus' prayer
'Our Father'

'This, then, is how you should pray:
"Our Father in heaven:
May your holy name be honoured;
may your Kingdom come;
may your will be done on earth as it is in heaven.
Give us today the food we need.
Forgive us the wrongs we have done,
as we forgive the wrongs that others have done to us.
Do not bring us to hard testing, but keep us safe from the Evil One."'
Matthew 6:9–13 (GNB)

This week we will be looking at the prayer that Jesus taught His disciples. It is a pattern that we can follow in our own daily prayers as well as saying it together in church. Look at the first line – 'Our Father'. Before Jesus came, the Jews had not often called God 'Father'. He had other names: the Lord, the Almighty, the King of glory, the Most High and many more, but Jesus taught us to call Him by the much more intimate name of 'Father'. It is much easier to talk to a loving Father than a God who is so far above us that we cannot reach Him.

Prayer:
Dear Father, I thank You that I am Your child and I can come to You at any time and talk to You about anything that is on my mind. Amen.

DAY 9

'May your holy name be honoured'

*D*ay and night [the angels] never stop singing: 'Holy, holy, holy, is the Lord God Almighty, who was, who is, and who is to come.'
'Our Lord and God! You are worthy
to receive glory, honour, and power.
For you created all things,
 and by your will they were given
existence and life.' *Revelation 4:8b,11 (GNB)*

Worship and adoration should always be part of our prayers. In heaven the angels worship God continually and we can join in, down here on earth, as we remember how great and mighty God is. Think about God today: He is the Creator of the universe, of the stars, the sun and moon, of all the wonderful trees and flowers and creatures in this world. He is full of glory and majesty. His power is beyond measure. He is holy. He is loving and compassionate, showing His love for us by sending His Son Jesus into the world to die for us so that we may be forgiven and enter into His presence. He is all-knowing; He sees all that happens in the world and He knows you – knows your thoughts and how you feel.

To think about:
You may like to make a list of all the things you can honour and praise God for. Then worship and praise Him today in your own words.

DAY 10

'May Your kingdom come'

*S*ome Pharisees asked Jesus when the Kingdom of God would come. His answer was, '... the Kingdom of God is within you.' *Luke 17:20–21 (GNB)*

'When the Son of Man comes as King and all the angels with him, he will sit on his royal throne, and the people of all the nations will be gathered before him ... Then the King will say to the people on his right, "Come, you that are blessed by my Father! Come and possess the kingdom which has been prepared for you ever since the creation of the world."'
Matthew 25:31–34 (GNB)

The kingdom of God is both present and future. Wherever God's will is perfectly done, where people acknowledge Him as King, *that* is where His kingdom is. Jesus said that the kingdom is within, or amongst, us. He meant that if we let God reign in our hearts, seeking to obey Him in all things, then we are part of His kingdom now.

But one day Jesus will come back to this earth again, not as a baby, as He did the first time, but as a King. He will judge between those who have loved Him and those who have not, and then He will reign for ever in His kingdom where His perfect will is always done.

Prayer:
Lord God, may Your kingdom dwell within me now. Come quickly, Lord, and reign on earth. Amen.

DAY 11

'May Your will be done'

'Those who accept my commandments and obey them are the ones who love me. My Father will love those who love me; I too will love them and reveal myself to them.'

Whoever loves me will obey my teaching. My Father will love him, and my Father and I will come to him and live with him. Whoever does not love me does not obey my teaching. And the teaching you have heard is not mine, but comes from the Father, who sent me.'
John 14:21,23–24 (GNB)

Obedience is sometimes produced by a fear of the one issuing the order. A child may fear punishment if he disobeys the teacher for example. But our relationship with God is not like that! Jesus made it very clear that we obey God because we love Him. And God's will, His teaching and His commandments are given to us because He loves us. God made us, so He knows the best way for us to live. All His commandments are given for our benefit. So when we pray, 'Your will be done', we are really asking God that all people will love Him so much that they will obey Him.

Prayer:
Lord, I love You. Please help me to obey Your teaching and to encourage others to love You too. Amen.

DAY 12

'Give us today the food we need'

'If you are God's Son, order these stones to turn into bread.' But Jesus answered, 'The scripture says, "Man cannot live on bread alone, but needs every word that God speaks."' Matthew 4:3–4 (GNB)

Jesus called his disciples to him and said, 'I feel sorry for these people, because they have been with me for three days and now have nothing to eat. I don't want to send them away without feeding them, for they might faint on their way home.' ... [Jesus] Then took the seven loaves and the fish ... [everyone] ate and had enough. Matthew 15:32,36a,37 (GNB)

These two scriptures show us that both spiritual food and natural food are necessary. God feeds our spirits with His Word in various ways – through our Bible readings, through church services and sometimes just through a quiet voice into our minds by His Holy Spirit.

In the second story Jesus was sorry for the crowds of people who were hungry and so He miraculously fed them all with bread and fish until they were satisfied.

God is concerned with both our spiritual and physical needs and we can ask Him to meet them. We should also understand that we have the responsibility to take and 'eat' what He gives us – His word and our daily food.

Prayer:
Thank You, Father, that You give me my daily food.
Amen.

DAY 13

'Forgive us ... as we forgive ... others.'

'If you forgive others the wrongs they have done to you, your Father in heaven will also forgive you. But if you do not forgive others, then your Father will not forgive the wrongs you have done.'
Matthew 6:14–15 (GNB)

When they came to the place called 'The Skull', they crucified Jesus there, and the two criminals, one on his right and the other on his left. Jesus said, 'Forgive them, Father! They don't know what they are doing.'
Luke 23:33–34 (GNB)

It is very difficult to forgive a person who has wronged or hurt us in some way. If we don't forgive, though, resentment can build up over the years and it affects our relationship with that person for ever. It also grieves God. Jesus told us to love one another and even to love our enemies.

If I find myself getting angry and unforgiving over a situation, it can be helpful to remember what Jesus suffered on the cross for me. He was unfairly accused, reviled, scorned, beaten and crucified. He did nothing to deserve such treatment – it was not His fault! Yet He forgave His tormentors and asked His Father to forgive them too.

Action:
Search your heart to see if there is any unforgiveness there towards anyone. Be willing, with God's help, to forgive and forget the offence they caused you.

DAY 14

'Do not bring us to hard testing'

Every test that you have experienced is the kind that normally comes to people. But God keeps His promise, and he will not allow you to be tested beyond your power to remain firm; at the time you are put to the test, he will give you the strength to endure it, and so provide you with a way out.
1 Corinthians 10:13 (GNB)

Put on all the armour that God gives you, so that you will be able to stand up against the Devil's evil tricks.
Ephesians 6:11 (GNB)

God does allow us to be tested at various times in our lives but He always gives us the ability and strength to stand up to the test and come through it. The tests are designed to build us up so that we learn more of God's power. We become more mature during difficult times when we have to rely on God's help rather than our own strength.

It is comforting to know that God will not take us through tests that are too hard for us but always gives us the means to cope.

Prayer:
Dear Father, I thank You that You have been with me all my life, helping me to come through times of testing and trial. Please keep me safe now. Amen.

The parables of Jesus

DAY 15

Jesus taught in parables

*J*esus spoke all these things to the crowd in parables; he did not say anything to them without using a parable. So was fulfilled what was spoken through the prophet:
'I will open my mouth in parables, I will utter things hidden since the creation of the world.' *Matthew 13:34–35*

The disciples came to [Jesus] and asked, 'Why do you speak to the people in parables?' He replied, 'The knowledge of the secrets of the kingdom of heaven has been given to you, but not to them.' *Matthew 13:10–11*

A parable is a story with a hidden meaning. Jesus spoke to the crowds in parables because they were not ready to understand the deep truths that He was teaching. The disciples, who really wanted to understand what Jesus was saying, would ask Him later when the crowds had gone away and Jesus would explain the meaning of the stories to them. Jesus wanted them to understand so that they could teach the gospel message to others.

We, too, can ask God to explain things that puzzle us. We cannot understand everything but as we stay close to Him, read His Word and talk to Him in prayer, then, we begin to understand His ways.

Prayer:
Father, there are many things I don't understand, but please make clear to me the things You want me to know. Amen.

DAY 16

The sower

'Listen! A farmer went out to sow his seed. As he was scattering the seed, some fell along the path, and the birds came and ate it up. Some fell on rocky places, where it did not have much soil. It sprang up quickly, because the soil was shallow. But when the sun came up, the plants were scorched, and they withered because they had no root. Other seed fell among thorns, which grew up and choked the plants, so that they did not bear grain. Still other seed fell on good soil. It came up, grew and produced a crop, multiplying thirty, sixty or even a hundred times.' *Mark 4:3–8*

Jesus explained this parable to His disciples: the seed is the Word of God. Some people are like the path; they hear the Word of God but don't understand so it is snatched away. Some are like the rocky ground; they hear the good news with joy but, when faced with trouble, they fall away. Others receive the Word and it begins to grow in their lives but the worries of this world choke the message and they, too, fall away. But those who hear the Word and keep it in their hearts are like the good soil. They will produce fruit for Him.

Action:
Ask yourself if there are any worries or distractions in your life that would hinder the growth of God's Word in your heart.

The Good Samaritan

'A man was going down from Jerusalem to Jericho, when he fell into the hands of robbers. They stripped him of his clothes, beat him and went away, leaving him half-dead. A priest happened to be going down the same road, and when he saw the man, he passed by on the other side. So, too, a Levite, when he came to the place and saw him, passed by on the other side. But a Samaritan, as he travelled, came where the man was; and when he saw him, he took pity on him. He went to him and bandaged his wounds, pouring on oil and wine. Then he put the man on his own donkey, brought him to an inn and took care of him.' *Luke 10:30–34*

In stopping to help the injured man the Samaritan was putting himself in danger. The robbers might have come back and attacked him as well. And the Jews despised the Samaritans – so why would a Samaritan put himself out to help a Jew?

But the good man didn't think of these things. He didn't consider his own safety. He saw a man in trouble and did all he could to help him. Jesus commended him for being a good neighbour and told His listeners to do the same.

Prayer:
Please help me, Lord, to be a good neighbour, giving help wherever I can. Amen.

DAY 18

The lost sheep

'What do you think? If a man owns a hundred sheep, and one of them wanders away, will he not leave the ninety-nine on the hills and go to look for the one who has wandered off? And if he finds it, I tell you the truth, he is happier about that one sheep than about the ninety-nine that did not wander off. In the same way your Father in heaven is not willing that any of these little ones should be lost.' *Matthew 18:12–14*

According to Matthew's Gospel Jesus had been talking to His disciples about the value of children when He told this parable. Every child and every person in the world is precious to God. He values you and every member of your family. Jesus is the Good Shepherd and everyone who believes in Him is counted among His sheep, so you are safe in His sheepfold. I wonder, though, if there are any in your family who have 'wandered off' like the sheep in this parable? It is comforting to know that Jesus cares so much about each one and will not cease to search for them until they are back in the fold.

Prayer:
Today think about those amongst your family or friends who have wandered away from God. Pray for them by name, asking that they will be brought safely back.

DAY 19

The house on the rock

'Therefore everyone who hears these words of mine and puts them into practice is like a wise man who built his house on the rock. The rain came down, the streams rose, and the winds blew and beat against that house; yet it did not fall, because it had its foundation on the rock. But everyone who hears these words of mine and does not put them into practice is like a foolish man who built his house on sand. The rain came down, the streams rose, and the wind blew and beat upon that house, and it fell with a great crash.' *Matthew 7:24–27*

When we build our lives on the Rock, Christ Jesus, and live according to His Word, then nothing can shake us. Jesus is not saying that we will not have trouble in our lives. Christians go through the same storms of life as other people – illness, bereavement, financial problems, difficulties with neighbours and so on – but in all these things we have the certainty that our heavenly Father is with us and will pull us through. We can stand firm on His promise, 'I am with you always' (Matt. 28:20) so we are not shaken by any calamity.

Prayer:
Dear Lord, You are my Rock; I build my life on You. I thank You that no matter what I may go through, You are with me and I will not be shaken. Amen.

The Pharisee and the tax collector

'Two men went up to the temple to pray, one a Pharisee and the other a tax collector. The Pharisee stood up and prayed about himself: "God, I thank you that I am not like other men – robbers, evil-doers, adulterers – or even like this tax collector. I fast twice a week and give a tenth of all I get."

But the tax collector stood at a distance. He would not even look up to heaven, but beat his breast and said, "God, have mercy on me, a sinner."

I tell you that this man, rather than the other, went home justified before God.' *Luke 18:10–14*

The Pharisee in this parable was a proud man, thinking he was more righteous than other people. The tax collector was humble, and confessed his sin before God and before other people. Jesus commended him for his humility.

As we grow older it is tempting to think we know better than the younger generation. Hopefully, we will have grown wiser in our old age but let us not be proud. We still need to confess our sins to God, to apologise to others if we have offended them and acknowledge humbly that we still have a lot to learn.

Prayer:
Dear Lord God, please show me if there is any sin in my life that I need to humbly confess to You today. Amen.

DAY 21

The silver coin

'Suppose a woman has ten silver coins and loses one. Does she not light a lamp, sweep the house and search carefully until she finds it? And when she finds it, she calls her friends and neighbours together and says, "Rejoice with me; I have found my lost coin." In the same way, I tell you, there is rejoicing in the presence of the angels of God over one sinner who repents.' *Luke 15:8–10*

Jesus told three parables about 'lost things' – the lost sheep, the lost coin and the lost (or prodigal) son showing in each one how much God cares about people who once believed in Jesus and followed Him, but have wandered away from the truth.

In the parable of the lost coin Jesus is emphasising how very precious that silver coin was to the lady. She turned her house upside down to look for it. It didn't matter to her that she still had nine other coins – she wanted the full quota of ten. She wanted her necklace to be complete. In the same way God cares about each one of His children. He wants His family to be complete. How precious we all are to Him! And even the angels in heaven rejoice when one sinner repents!

Prayer:
Father, please show me how I can help You search for and find those of Your children who have wandered away from You. Amen.

DAY 22

God's Comfort
Abraham and Sarah

So Abram left [his country], as the Lord had told him ... He took his wife Sarai, his nephew Lot, all the possessions they had accumulated and the people they had acquired in Haran, and they set out for the land of Canaan, and they arrived there. *Genesis 12:1,4–5*

Sarah lived to be a hundred and twenty-seven years old. She died at Kiriath Arba (that is, Hebron) in the land of Canaan, and Abraham went to mourn for Sarah and to weep over her. *Genesis 23:1–2*

Abraham and his wife Sarai, later called Sarah, were already old when God called them to leave their home country and travel to an unknown land. Together they went through hardships and testing times, family problems, wars and natural disasters. Together they shared the joy of a son, Isaac, born miraculously in Sarah's old age.

So it must have been a great grief to Abraham when his beloved wife died. He wept and mourned, as any husband would have done.

As we grow older, inevitably we begin to lose people close to us and it is always a great sadness. In our mourning, though, we can take comfort in knowing that God understands our sadness and draws close to us with His comforting presence.

Prayer:
Dear Lord, thank You that You understand how I feel in times of grief and You will comfort me. Amen.

DAY 23

Death of Abraham

Abraham left everything he owned to Isaac. But while he was still living, he gave gifts to the sons of his concubines and sent them away from his son Isaac to the land of the east. Altogether, Abraham lived a hundred and seventy-five years. Then Abraham breathed his last and died at a good old age, an old man and full of years; and he was gathered to his people. His sons Isaac and Ishmael buried him in the cave of Machpelah near Mamre ... Genesis 25:5-9

The Bible is a very practical book, covering every aspect of human life and death. At the end of his long life Abraham left everything he owned to his son and heir, Isaac. It is good to make a will; things are easier for the family then. But Abraham also gave generously to his other sons while he was alive and, realising that they could cause trouble for Isaac later, he sent them away to live in another land.

It is heartening to read that Isaac and Ishmael, who had been at enmity with each other during their lives, came together to bury their father. Let us do all we can in our own families to make things easy and keep them together.

Prayer:
Dear Father, thank You for my family. Please show me what I can do to bring harmony, love and practical help to my loved ones. Amen.

DAY 24

Jesus and His mother

*N*ear the cross of Jesus stood his mother, his mother's sister, Mary the wife of Clopas, and Mary Magdalene. When Jesus saw his mother there, and the disciple whom he loved standing nearby, he said to his mother, 'Dear woman, here is your son', and to the disciple, 'Here is your mother.' From that time on, this disciple took her into his home. *John 19:25–27*

In the midst of His unspeakable suffering, nailed to a cross, Jesus showed His care for His mother. Knowing that, as the eldest son in the family, He would not be able to look after her in her old age, He provided for her future. It is an amazing example of the love of God. Jesus, the Son of God, showed us how to ignore our own sufferings and act with compassion towards others. John referred to himself here as, 'the disciple whom Jesus loved' and no doubt Jesus chose him to look after Mary because John was a loving man and would understand the trauma that she was going through at that time.

Jesus understands our sufferings because He, Himself, has suffered and He longs to look after us just as He looked after His own mother.

Prayer:
Thank You, Jesus, for showing me how You looked after Your mother. I trust You to look after me, too, and ask that, like you, I may have concern for others. Amen.

DAY 25

Comfort

*P*raise be to the God and Father of our Lord Jesus Christ, the Father of compassion and the God of all comfort, who comforts us in all our troubles, so that we can comfort those in any trouble with the comfort we ourselves have received from God. *2 Corinthians 1:3-4*

But God, who comforts the downcast, comforted us by the coming of Titus, and not only by his coming but also by the comfort you had given him. *2 Corinthians 7:6-7*

God has not promised us an easy life; we all go through difficult times, but He has promised to be with us always. God's very presence comforts us in all our troubles and sufferings. Just as it is good to have an understanding person with us when we go through difficulties, so it is doubly good to know that God is with us and that He understands what we are going through better than even our nearest and dearest.

But notice the second part of this scripture – we are comforted so that we can comfort others. God's comfort is not a selfish thing that we keep to ourselves; it is for sharing.

Action:
Think about those around you today. Is there anyone whom you can help? Anyone who needs comfort or a word of loving compassion? Pray that you will be sensitive to the needs of others.

DAY 26

David and the child

*A*fter Nathan had gone home, the LORD struck the child that Uriah's wife had borne to David, and he became ill. David pleaded with God for the child … On the seventh day the child died.
2 Samuel 12:15–16,18a

David … went into the house of the LORD and worshipped. Then he went to his own house and at his request they served him food, and he ate. His servants asked him, 'Why are you acting this way?' … He answered, 'While the child was still alive, I fasted and wept. But now that he is dead why should I fast?' … Then David comforted his wife Bathsheba. *2 Samuel 12:20–23,24*

It is always particularly distressing when a child dies. King David was a loving father and he did all he could for his seriously ill son, fasting and praying, calling out to God to heal the child. This time, however, God did not heal and the child died. Some would then have railed against God, becoming bitter, disillusioned and angry but David wasn't like that. Instead he accepted the situation, worshipped God and then went to comfort his wife. God understands our grief and will comfort and sustain us through it.

Prayer:
Please help me, Lord, to be able to share with others the comfort that You give to me. Amen.

Naomi and Ruth

*I*n the days when the judges ruled, there was a famine in the land, and a man from Bethlehem in Judah, together with his wife and two sons, went to live for a while in the country of Moab. The man's name was Elimelech, his wife's name Naomi, and the names of his two sons were Mahlon and Kilion ... Now Elimelech, Naomi's husband, died, and she was left with her two sons. They married Moabite women, one named Orpah and the other Ruth. After they had lived there about ten years, both Mahlon and Kilion also died, and Naomi was left without her two sons and her husband. *Ruth 1:1–2a,3–5*

Naomi felt bitter, having lost her husband and two grown-up sons in a foreign land. This is a heart-warming story, however, as it unfolds. Naomi's daughter-in-law, Ruth, insisted on staying with her when she decided to travel back to her own country. It cannot have been easy for Ruth, but she remained loving and supportive of the older woman, and God rewarded her by leading her to a second husband. Ruth and Boaz became ancestors of King David and further down the line, of Jesus Himself. In this story, God brought good out of a tragic situation, as He often does.

Prayer:
Help me to trust You, Lord, when things are difficult. I want to remain faithful to You, whatever my situation. Amen.

God's promise

*P*raise be to the God and Father of our Lord Jesus Christ! In his great mercy he has given us new birth into a living hope through the resurrection of Jesus Christ from the dead, and into an inheritance that can never perish, spoil or fade – kept in heaven for you, who through faith are shielded by God's power until the coming of the salvation that is ready to be revealed in the last time. In this you greatly rejoice, though … you may have had to suffer grief in all kinds of trials. *1 Peter 1:3–6*

We who trust in God know that death is not the end! Jesus rose from the dead and in so doing He conquered death and made it possible for us also to live for ever with Him in heaven. There is a place reserved in heaven for you! One day you will see Jesus face to face and experience His love in an amazing way – far greater than on this earth – far greater than you can imagine. That thought is comforting as we come nearer to the end of our own lives and also as we experience the loss of loved ones who trust in God.

Prayer:
Lord Jesus, thank You for giving Your life for me on the cross. Thank You too that You have gone before me to heaven to prepare a place for me there. Amen.

Sing praises to God

DAY 29

My heart is steadfast, O God;
   I will sing and make music with all my soul.
Awake, harp and lyre!
   I will awaken the dawn.
I will praise you, O Lord, among the nations;
   I will sing of you among the peoples.
For great is your love, higher than the heavens;
   your faithfulness reaches to the skies.
Be exalted, O God, above the heavens,
   and let your glory be over all the earth
Psalm 108:1–5

As we read this psalm we can imagine David playing his harp at break of day and singing aloud with joy to the Lord. He is full of praise to God and not afraid of letting people know what is in his heart. He wants, not only to express his admiration to his Lord, but to tell out to others too how great, how loving, how faithful God is. I wonder if we are so forthcoming with our praise? Or are we perhaps a little fearful of what others may think of us? God is worthy of our praise, all the time, every day.

Action:
If you are able, read this psalm aloud today and make it your own hymn of praise to our great and wonderful God.

DAY 30

Sing for joy

Come, let us sing for joy to the LORD;
 let us shout aloud to the Rock of our salvation.
Let us come before him with thanksgiving
 and extol him with music and song.
For the LORD is the great God,
 the great King above all gods.
In his hand are the depths of the earth,
 and the mountain peaks belong to him.
The sea is his, for he made it,
 and his hands formed the dry land.
Psalm 95:1–5

Another wonderful psalm of praise and thanksgiving! The psalmist is full of joy as he considers God's nature and provision. God is the God of salvation – the One who saves His people. The psalmist didn't know then that God's Son, Jesus, was to come into the world to save us from our sin, but we know now. He praises God as the great King above all other gods. We know that one day Jesus will come back to this earth to reign as King. As we think about that we are full of praise too!

Praise:
Lord God, great God, I praise You today with joy in my heart for who You are – mighty, loving, compassionate Father. Thank You for sending Jesus into this world. Thank You, Jesus, that one day You are coming back. Amen.